Marriage AIN'T FOR WIMPS

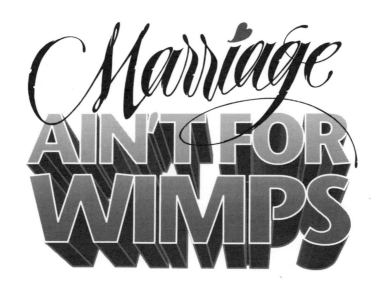

Marriage AIN'T FOR WIMPS

The Best Cartoons from *Marriage Partnership*

RON R. LEE • EDITOR

ZondervanPublishingHouse
Grand Rapids, Michigan

A Division of HarperCollinsPublishers

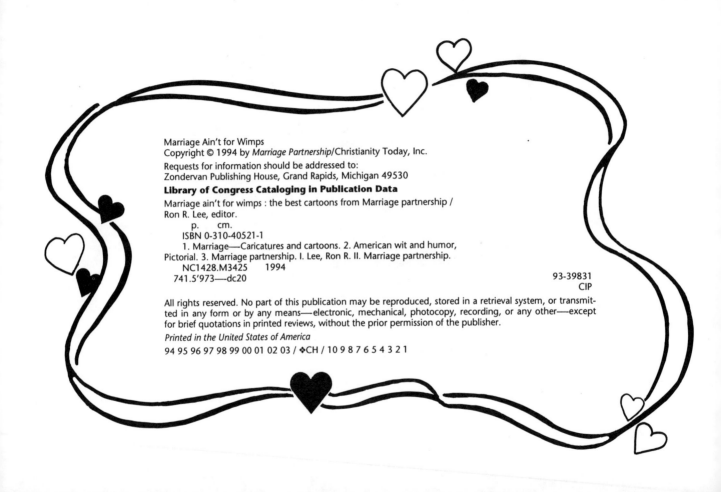

Marriage Ain't for Wimps
Copyright © 1994 by *Marriage Partnership*/Christianity Today, Inc.

Requests for information should be addressed to:
Zondervan Publishing House, Grand Rapids, Michigan 49530

Library of Congress Cataloging in Publication Data

Marriage ain't for wimps : the best cartoons from Marriage partnership /
Ron R. Lee, editor.
  p. cm.
  ISBN 0-310-40521-1
  1. Marriage—Caricatures and cartoons. 2. American wit and humor,
Pictorial. 3. Marriage partnership. I. Lee, Ron R. II. Marriage partnership.
  NC1428.M3425 1994
  741.5'973—dc20

                      93-39831
                       CIP

Printed in the United States of America

94 95 96 97 98 99 00 01 02 03 / ❖CH / 10 9 8 7 6 5 4 3 2 1

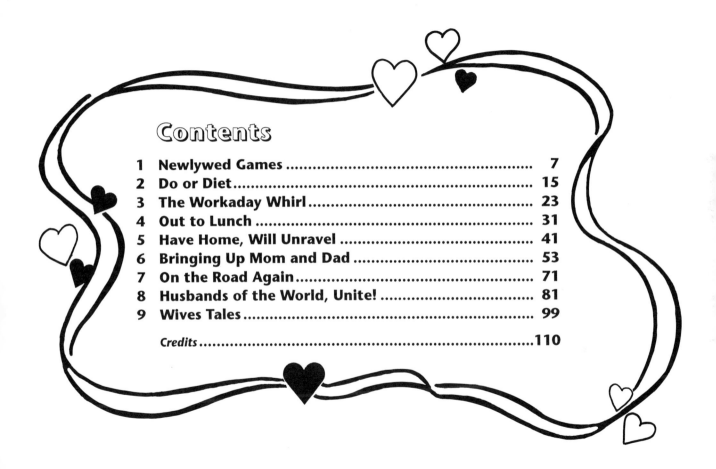

Contents

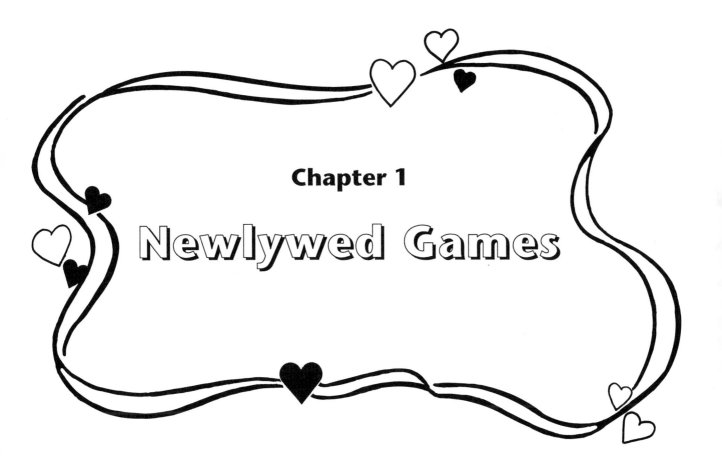

Chapter 1

Newlywed Games

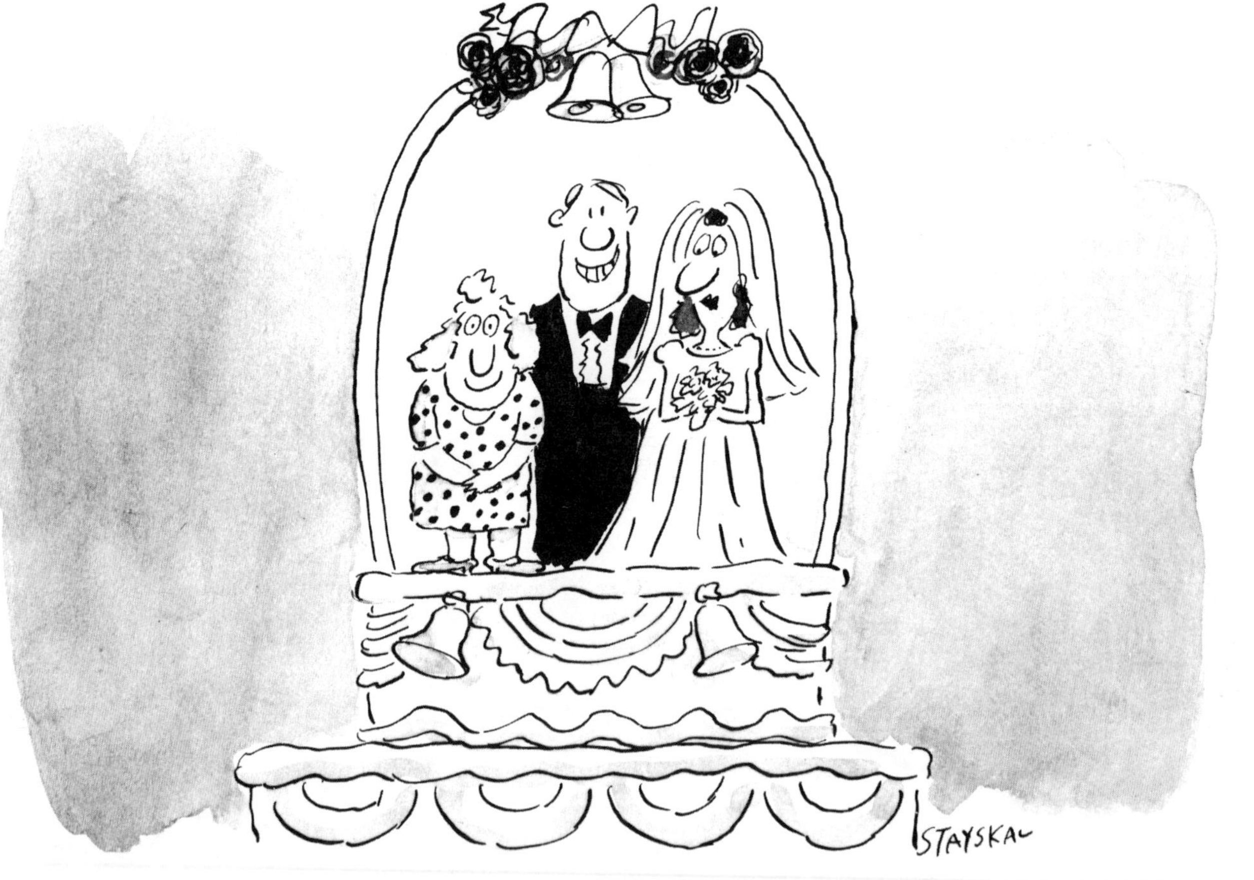
STAYSKAL

Despite his bad back, Wayne made sure
his bride was carried over the threshold.

9

After his new bride took off her makeup, Benny's
worst fears were realized!

10

"So, as you embark on the sea of life . . ."

It's important for newlyweds to be diplomatic when
deciding whether to spend Christmas at his parents' or hers.

"Of course I'm pig-headed!
You knew that when you married me!"

"I don't know where Roger could have gone, Mother.
He was right here when you knocked."

Chapter 2

Do or Diet

"Harriet's diet? Coming along just fine. Easy as pie!
Piece of cake! Bowl of cherries!"

"Give it up, Emmett . . . gorging yourself with fiber now won't undo what the doctor says you've done to your body the past 55 years."

How to make your wife HYSTERICAL.

"Freeze . . . DIET POLICE . . . put down that cold
pasta salad, lady, nice and slow and
nobody'll get hurt . . ."

19

"If you ask me, Gloria, you're going a bit too far with this diet."

"Something to always remember . . . never unplug Daddy's treadmill while he's running on it."

"Madge is on that 'twenty glasses of water a day' diet."

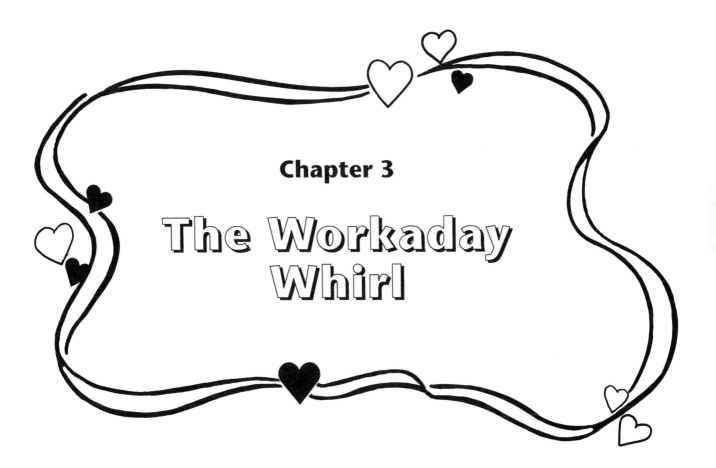

Chapter 3

The Workaday Whirl

"Davy! You know I hate it when you bring
your work home with you!"

"Your wife just called . . . she said you left your briefcase next to the dog's dish."

25

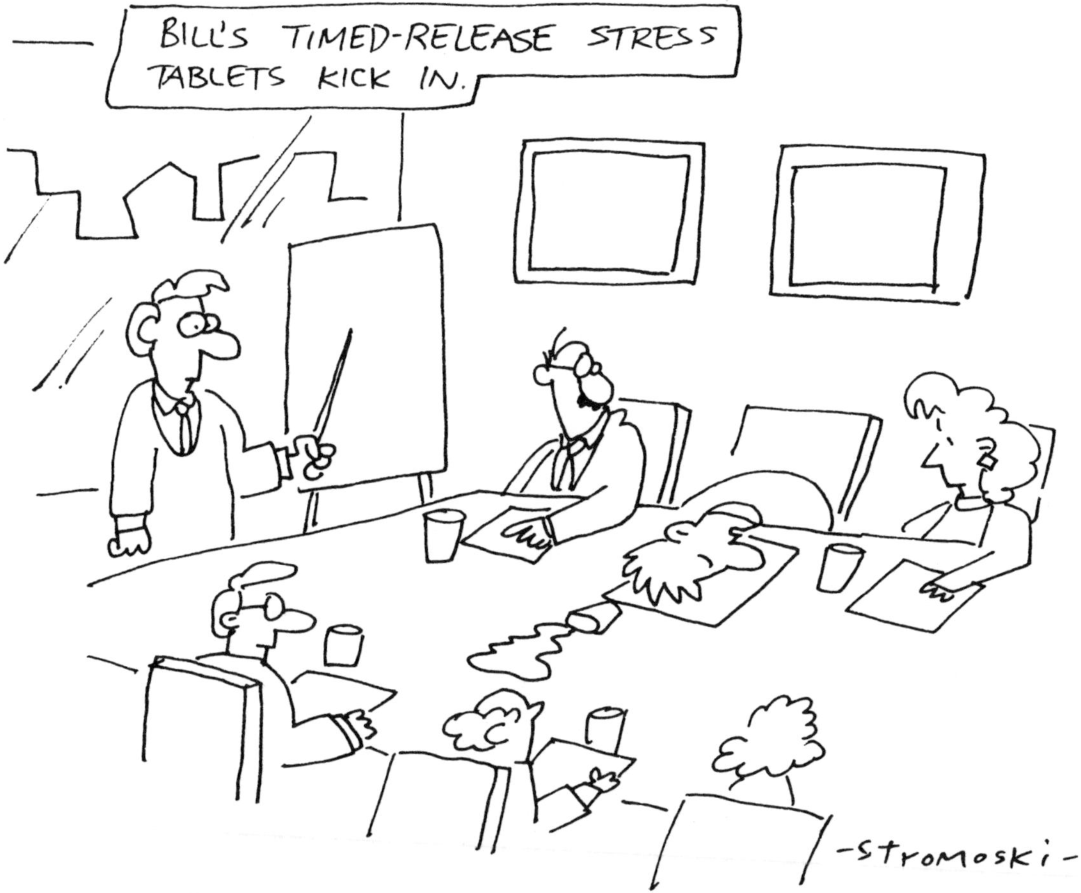
BILL'S TIMED-RELEASE STRESS TABLETS KICK IN.
-STROMOSKI-

"My wife . . . she's always putting these little surprises
in my lunchpail . . ."

28   "How about a nice walk before dinner to help you unwind?"

"He's out working in the garden."

Chapter 4

Out to Lunch

"I'm Peter and I'll be your waiter tonight. This is Norm, he'll be your dishwasher tonight. And this is Al, he'll take your leftovers out to the dumpster tonight."

"It's a low-cholesterol hotdog. Actually, it's a carrot in a bun."

"Oh, Boston *Cream* Pie. I thought the recipe
said Boston *Clam* Pie."

"Tommy! How many times have I told you
not to play with your food?!"

"Can you believe it? George a Cajun chef? And all these years
I thought we were just eating burnt hamburgers . . ."

"I have to go now, Bernice . . . Floyd wants something."

"I just love it when
you're naughty, Mel!"

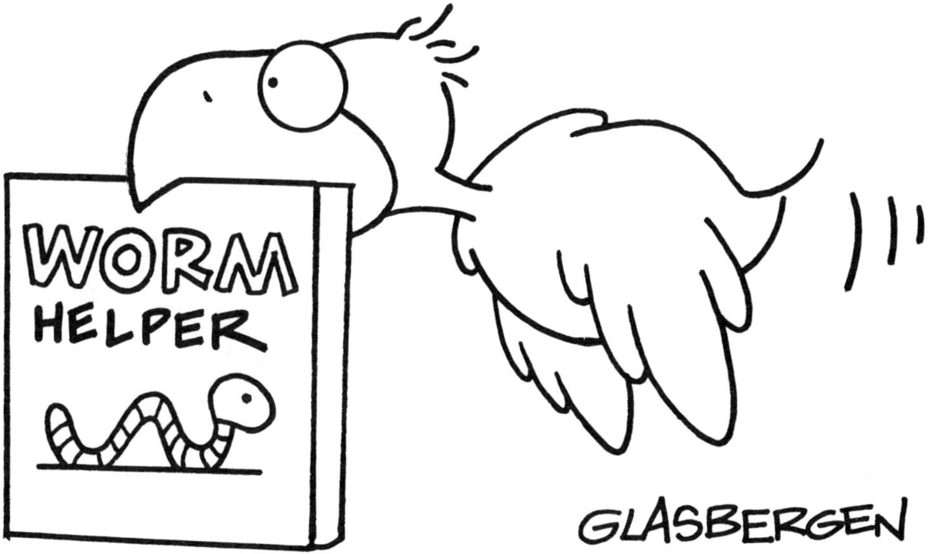
WORM
HELPER
GLASBERGEN

In spite of their hectic schedules, Sue and Bob
always looked forward to their weekly date night.

Chapter 5

Have Home, Will Unravel

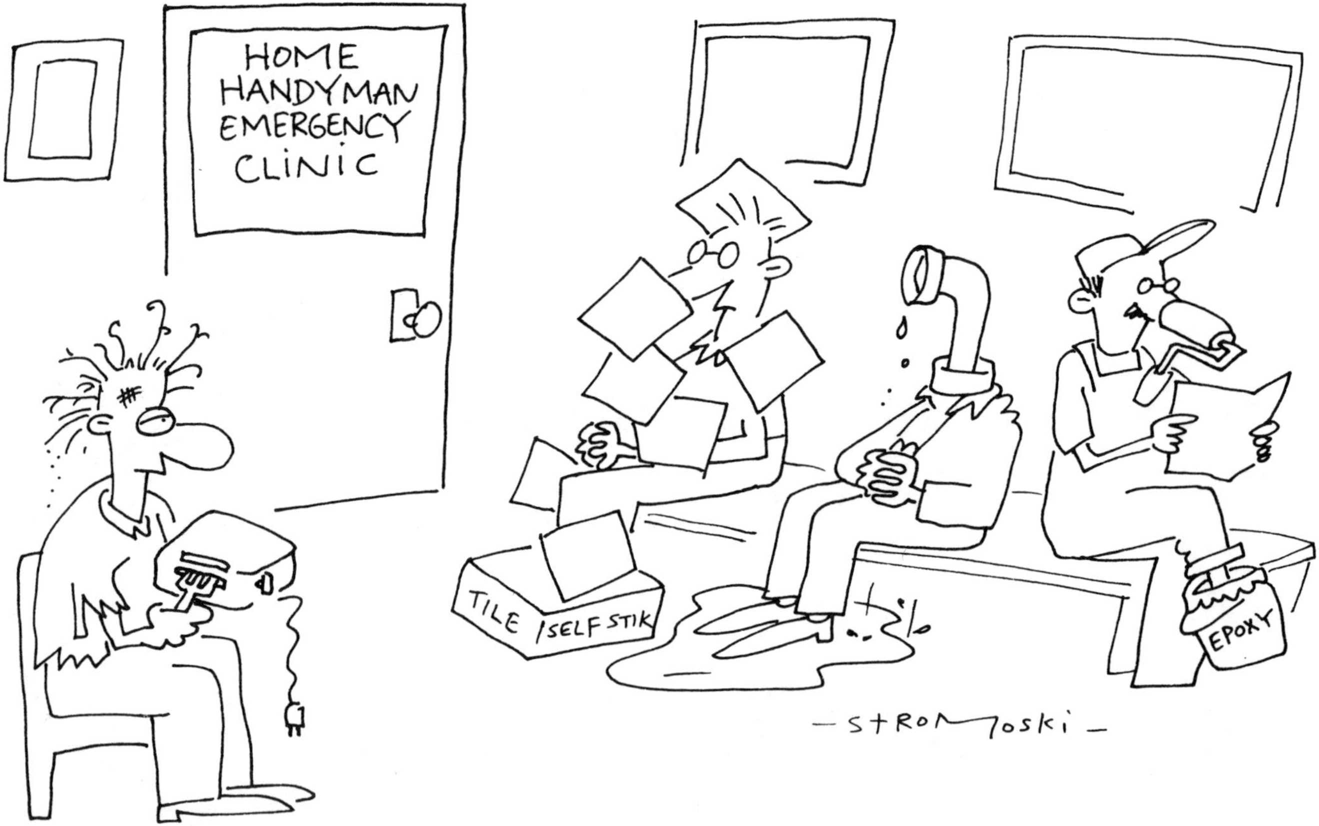
HOME HANDYMAN EMERGENCY CLINIC
TILE
SELF STIK
EPOXY
-STROMOSKI-

"Haven't you unclogged that sink yet?!"

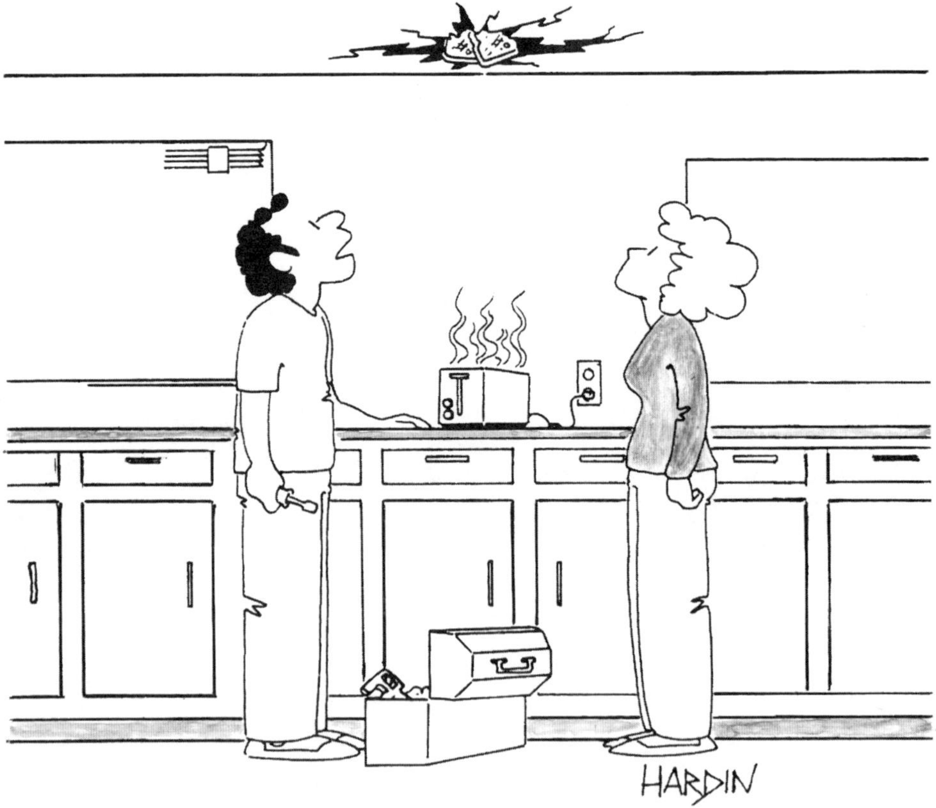
HARDIN

"At least it pops up now."

"He'll be here in a minute—he's just putting up
some shelves in the kitchen."

45

"It never fails, first we have an earthquake
and then it snows."

"Lucy, I think we need to have a little talk
about this stenciling project of yours."

47

"I made the chicken salad . . . my husband made the chair . . ."

Male fulfillment—a full pegboard.

"It's nice, Virgil, but where's the closet space?"

"Just a quiet afternoon at home. I'm doing some housework and Stan is trying out his new mulcher."

Chapter 6

Bringing Up
Mom and Dad

"So, then Father Flannegan says to the judge, 'There are no bad boys—only guilty parents.'"

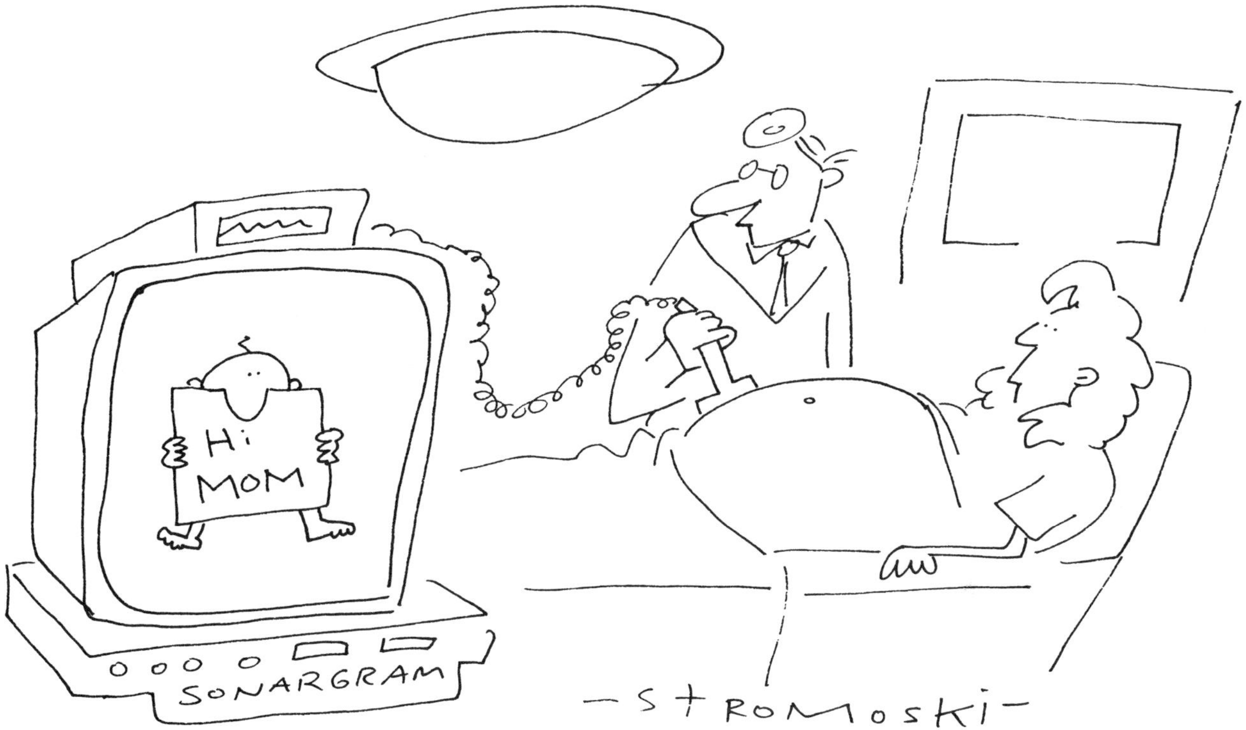
Hi
MOM
SONARGRAM
-STROMOSKI-

"My! What a good burp *that* was! Let's
have one more now!"

"Honey, better check the umbrella stand!"

"Did one of you forget a jumbo burger
and a small fry?"

"The wife still visiting her folks, is she, Fred?"

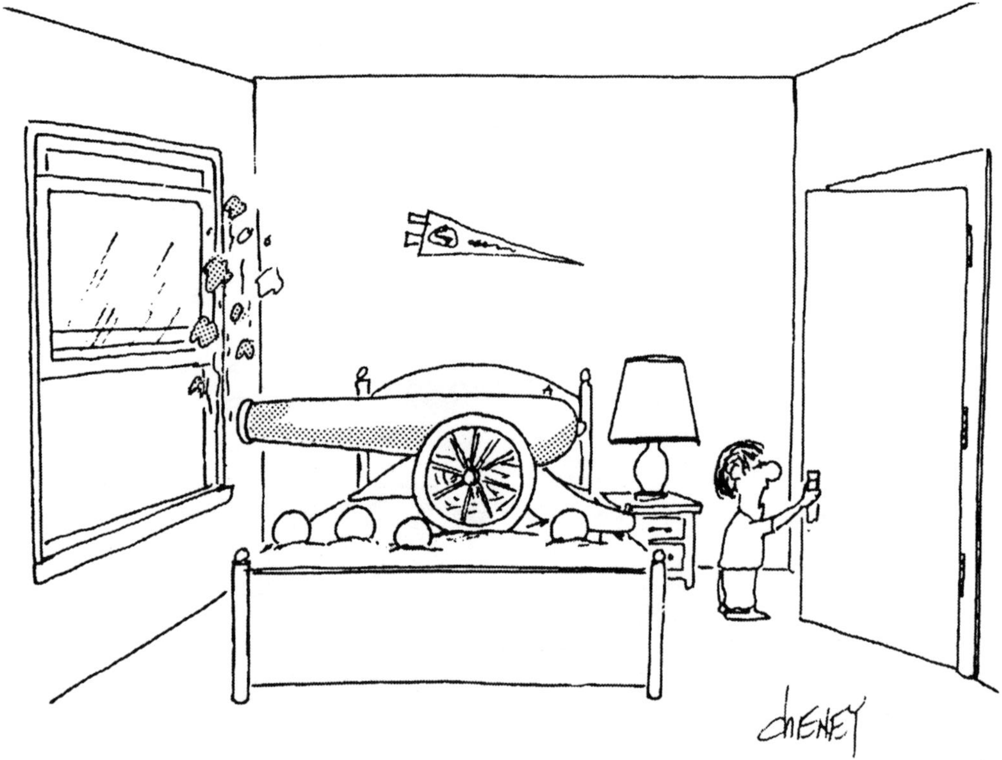

"Nothing, Mom!"

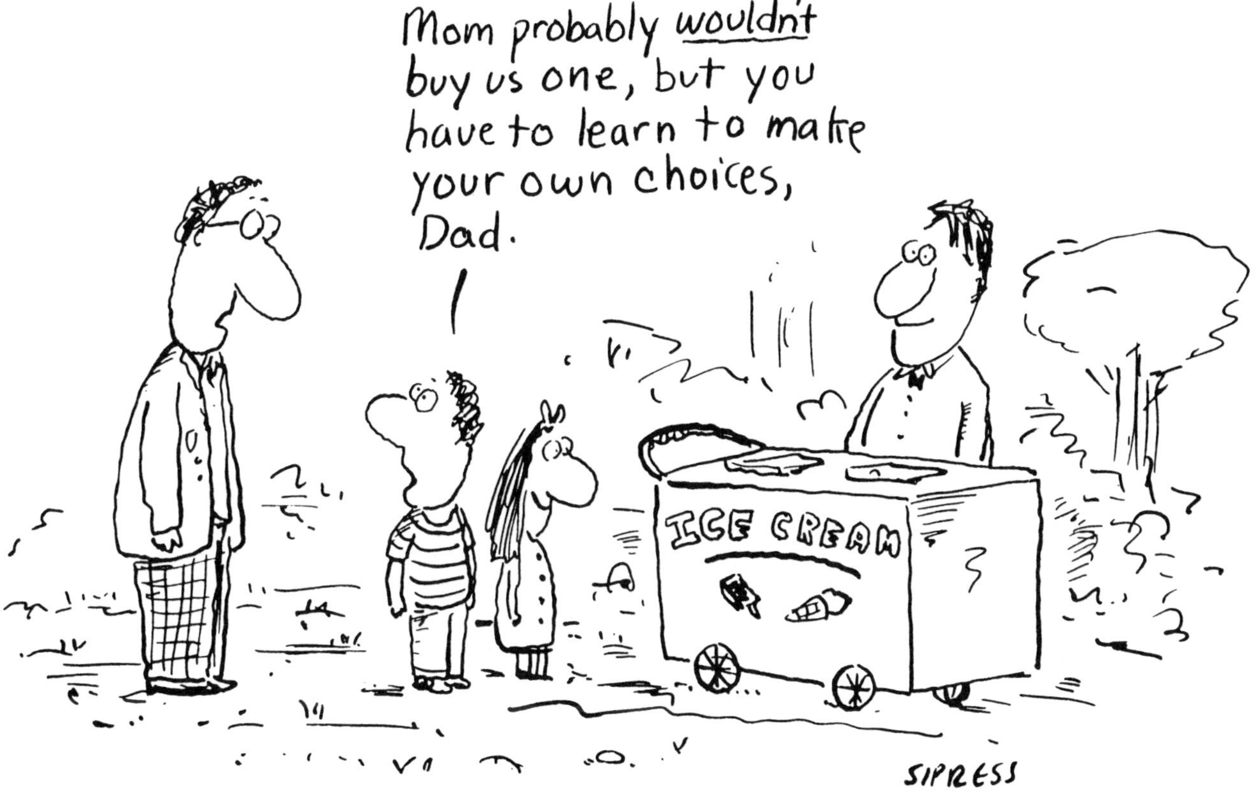
Mom probably wouldn't buy us one, but you have to learn to make your own choices, Dad.
ICE CREAM
SIPRESS

"These are my parents—nice people,
but totally computer-illiterate."

"Do you think it will ever get as cold
as it did when Dad was our age?"

"Why do teenagers always think they have to be different?"

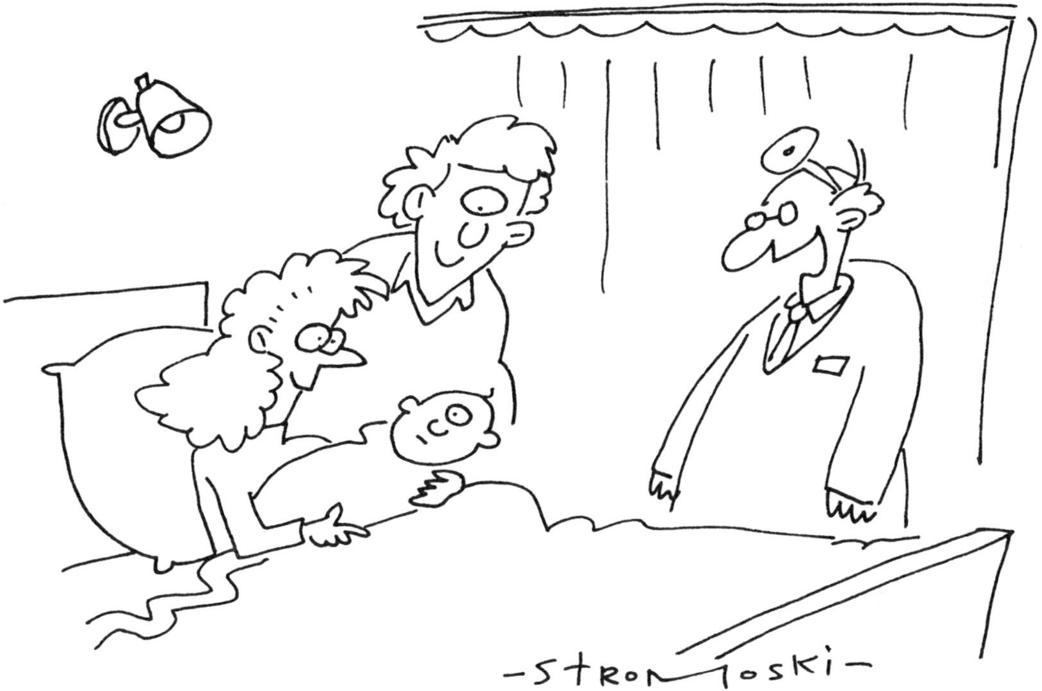
-STROMOSKI-

"He's got his father's eye."

"Today I was voted most popular girl in school.
Now everyone hates me."

"Considering they're going to have to feed him,
I'd say this tuition looks darn reasonable."

"Having completed your performance review,
I'd recommend a parenting workshop."

"This is Dave's first time changing the baby's diaper."

Chapter 7

On the Road Again

"Admit it, Harold . . . we're lost!"

"Are you kidding? Buy a station wagon?
Those things get lousy mileage!"

"Harold, I *told* you to stay out of the sun—
you burn so easily!"

GLASBERGEN

74

"Hey, listen to this . . . 'In case of a bear encounter remain motionless and play dead' . . . They actually believe this junk!"

"I hope we didn't forget anything, Stella."

"If we economize we can afford our dream vacation.
First we paddle a rowboat to Europe . . ."

"Looks like another great day
for some quality time, honey."

Martha and the kids having gone visiting for the weekend,
it wasn't long before Richard was up to his usual mischief.

Chapter 8

Husbands of the World, Unite

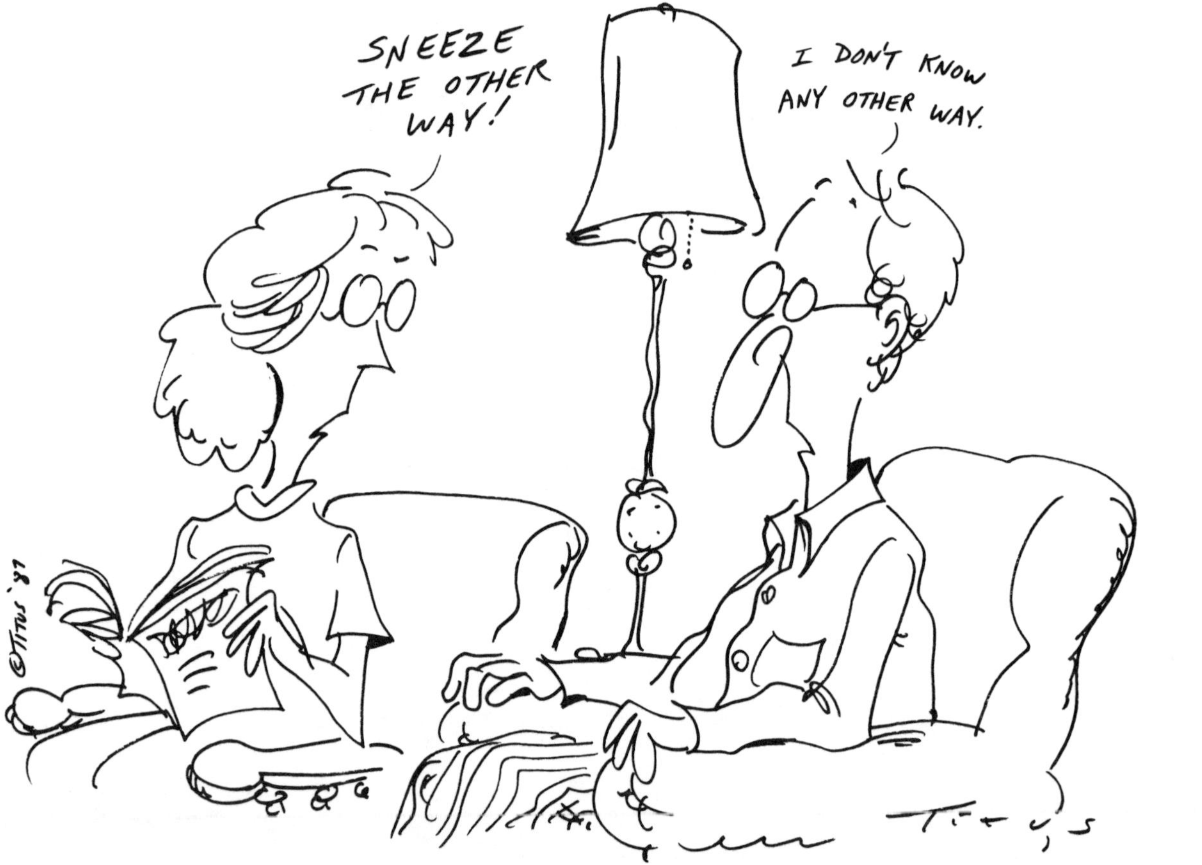
SNEEZE THE OTHER WAY!
I DON'T KNOW ANY OTHER WAY.

"Notice anything different?"

"New car or not, Harold,
you can't keep the bugs off the grille forever!"

"I think I slept wrong last night."

"Say, I notice that hair thickener you bought
is beginning to work!"

"Enough about love and marriage,
let's talk about football."

"Actually, this van can't guarantee family happiness.
That's only an option on the LX model."

"The batteries to the remote are getting weak."

"Waddaya mean 'what is it'? It's a lava lamp."

"Maybe some night we could go
to a movie, huh?"

"How can you say I'm not romantic?
Last night I blinked 'I love you' in Morse code!"

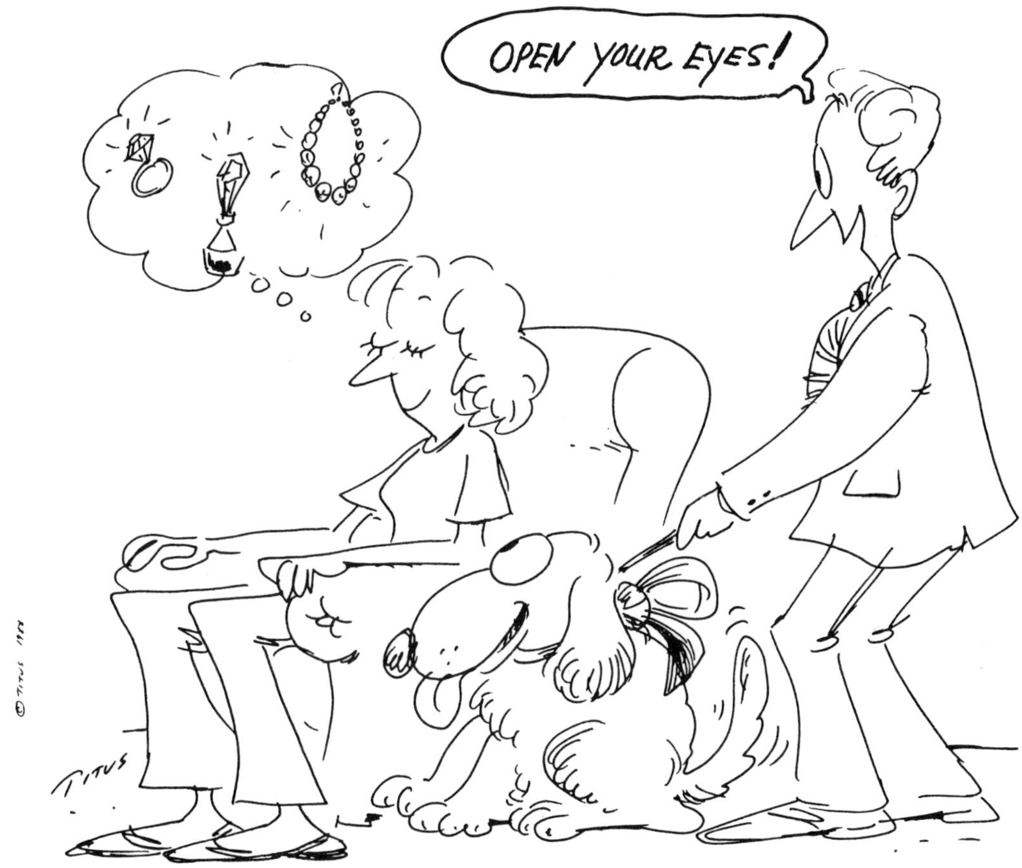
OPEN YOUR EYES!
TITUS

"When I said, 'Tonight's the night,' George, what I meant was to take out the garbage!"

"Federal Bureau of Feelings, sir. It seems that last night you neglected to ask your wife how her day was. You have the right to remain silent."

"... What? ... my transmission?! ... how much?! ... nine hundred dollars?!!"

"Helloooo, honey, your Love Machine is
home for yoooooou!"

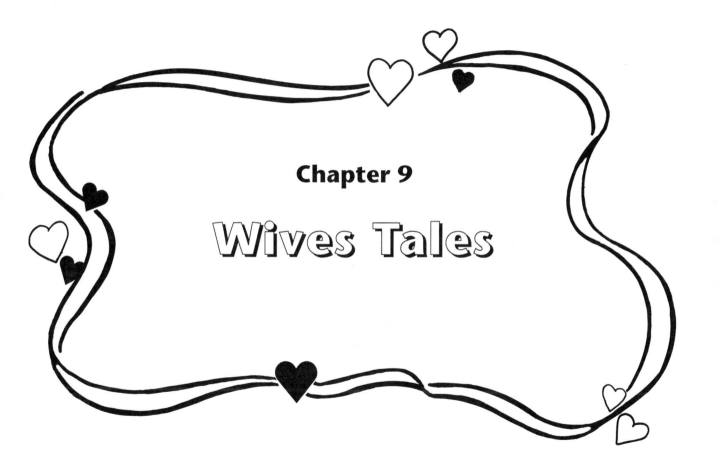

Chapter 9

Wives Tales

"I brought you the strongest pain reliever you can get without a prescription—me!"

"Would you mind, Arthur? There's a spider near the sink."

"I'm ready, dear!"

. . . You're twenty minutes late, and your wife asks,
"How does my hair look, honey?"

"For Pete's sake! I'm all ready to go
and you're not even dressed yet!"

"Could I have just a *smiiiiidge* more room, dear?"

Busíno

"You never take me any place anymore."

"Did you remember the mousse?"

"Strange . . . I suddenly have this overwhelming urge
to go home and pick my socks up off the bedroom floor!"

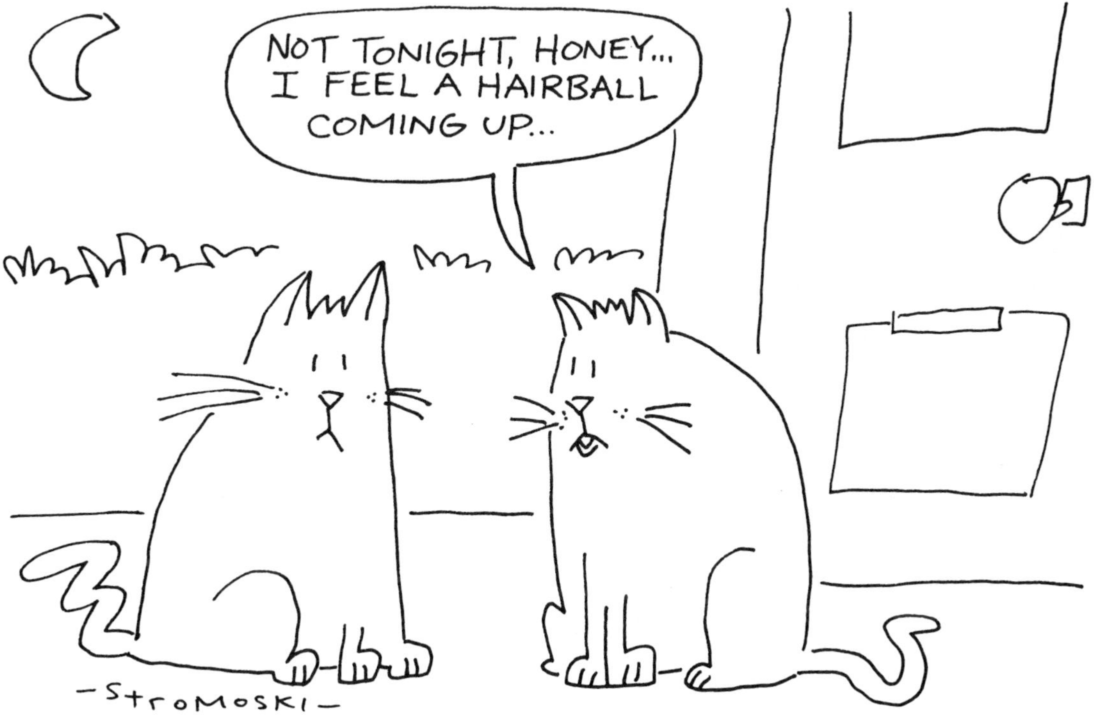
NOT TONIGHT, HONEY... I FEEL A HAIRBALL COMING UP...
-STROMOSKI-

Credits

The cartoons on pages 21, 25, 29, 46, 60, 72, 79, 83, 95, 101 and108 were reprinted with permission from THE SATURDAY EVENING POST.

The cartoon on page 61 is reprinted from IT'S A DAD'S LIFE by David Sipress. Copyright © 1989 by David Sipress. Used by permission of the New American Library, a division of Penguin Books USA Inc.

The cartoons on pages 20 and 45: Copyright © Punch/Rothco.

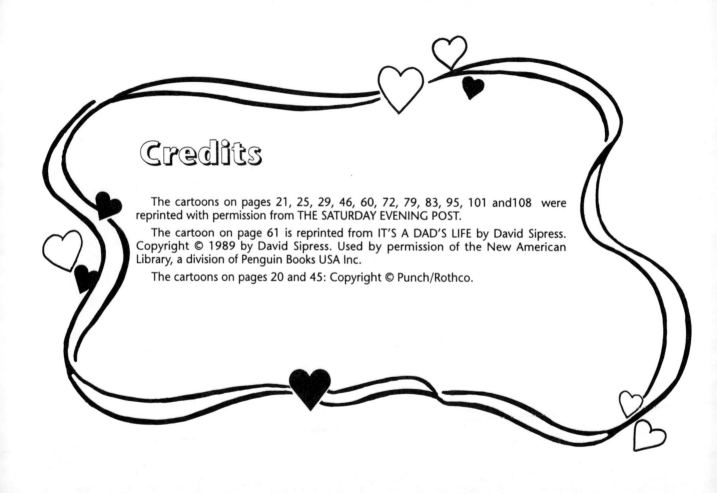